GW00632156

cocktails prepared by
laurent giraud-dumas
of the lanesborough hotel

with photography by
laura hodgson

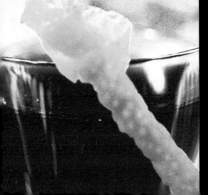

cocktails

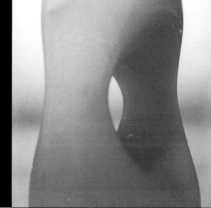

kyle cathie limited

for I.J.A. – the conservative cocktail drinker

First published in Great Britain 1998 by
Kyle Cathie Limited
20 Vauxhall Bridge Road
London SW1V 2SA

10 9 8 7 6 5 4 3 2 1

ISBN 1 85626 312 6

All rights reserved. No reproduction, copy or transmission of this publication may be made
without written permission. No paragraph of this publication may be reproduced, copied or
transmitted save with the written permission or in accordance with the provision of the
Copyright Act 1956 (as amended). Any person who does any unauthorised act in relation
to this publication may be liable to criminal prosecution and civil claims for damages.

Text © 1998 Kyle Cathie Limited
Photography © 1998 Laura Hodgson

Kyle Cathie Limited is hereby identified as the author of this work in accordance with
Section 77 of the Copyright, Designs and Patents Act 1988

A Cataloguing In Publication record for this title is available from the British Library.

Edited by Kirsten Abbott & Kate Oldfield
Designed by Button Design Company
Production by Lorraine Baird

Colour reproduction by SX Composing
Printed and bound in Singapore by Tien Wah Press

presentation is everything

contents

contents

the raw material

The minimalist cocktail drinker could entertain simply with one bottle each of vodka, gin and white or dark rum, but the cocktail addict's drinks cabinet expands with their repertoire. A collection of tequila, cointreau, kahlúa, brandy or cognac, galliano, baileys and bourbon can produce just about any cocktail. And a bottle of blue curaçao, crème de menthe or pisang ambon indicates a true connoisseur. For dashes and top ups, you will also need Angostura bitters, grenadine, lime cordial, exotic fruit juices and mixers such as soda or cola. Remember that some of these liquids are used as much for their glorious colours as for their taste. Before embarking on an evening of cocktails, make sure you have all vital ingredients to hand – you never know when a 'kiss me kate' will lead to 'sex on the beach' 'down under'.

equip yourself

If you have no other implement for cocktail making, you must have a shaker. Other necessary utensils are a mixing glass, a bar spoon, a blender, a strainer and a measure. If you do not have a proper measure use a shot glass or the lid of a bottle. All liquid quantities in this book are given in measures (although all that is important to remember is, whatever you use, be consistent in your measurements – when making a cocktail for a lot of people use a measure more suitable for larger quantities). Of course, the measures can be adjusted according to the potency required!

A range of good glassware is essential. Aim for a collection of tumblers, highballs, solid little shot glasses, balloons, cocktail glasses, (known also as martini glasses after their most famous liquid lodger), and, of course, elegant champagne flutes and coupes.

life on the edge

Indulge in the aesthetics of cocktails: colour, glassware, garnish. It's all about looks. Try the brilliant hues of a 'blue lagoon', the intense shades of a 'japanese slipper' or the subtle clarity of a 'vodkatini'.

But don't limit yourself to all things traditional. The shape of the glass adds another dimension to a cocktail – look out for unusually shaped glasses in markets and antique shops.

Let garnish too be the voice of self-expression. Sculpt a cherry into a heart shape, slice a star fruit, zest a lime. Use your imagination! Umbrellas and swizzle sticks have never been more hip. For the ultimate in adornment set your cocktail alight (see pages 24 and 40).

For further ideas on the art of cocktail making see laurent's tips on page 62.

sloe gin fizz

2 sloe gin

1 lemon juice

teaspoon sugar

egg white

soda

lemon, blueberry or gooseberry to garnish

.....................shaker...strainer...highball..................

SHAKE THE SUGAR, LEMON JUICE, SLOE GIN AND EGG WHITE.
STRAIN INTO AN ELEGANT HIGHBALL. TOP UP WITH SODA.

after dinner

1 cognac

$^1/_2$ kalhúa

$^1/_2$ frangelico

dash crème de menthe

cream

grated chocolate to garnish

..........mixing glass...shaker...strainer...cocktail glass.....

IN A MIXING GLASS STIR THE COGNAC, KALHÚA AND
FRANGELICO THEN STRAIN INTO A COCKTAIL GLASS. SHAKE
THE CRÈME DE MENTHE AND CREAM WITH TWO ICE CUBES,
STRAIN AND SLIDE OVER THE BACK OF A BAR SPOON.

japanese slipper

"Turning Japanese
I think
I'm turning
Japanese,
I really think so"

1 tequila

1 midori

dash lime or lemon juice

..........shaker...strainer...sugar-rimmed martini glass.....

BRISKLY SHAKE THE INGREDIENTS WITH ICE AND STRAIN
INTO A MARTINI GLASS. FOR SUGAR RIM SEE PAGE 63.

pousse cafe

$^{1}/_{2}$ grenadine

$^{1}/_{2}$ green chartreuse

$^{1}/_{2}$ galliano

$^{1}/_{2}$ kummel

$^{1}/_{2}$ cognac

.....bar spoon...large shot glass.....

IN PRECISE ORDER, POUR LAYERS OF FIRST GRENADINE,
THEN GREEN CHARTREUSE, GALLIANO, KUMMEL AND
FINALLY COGNAC OVER THE BACK OF A BAR SPOON.

batida

2 rum

1 coconut cream

pineapple juice

4 fresh strawberries

starfruit, cherry and mint leaf to garnish

......................................*balloon glass...blender*......................................

IN A BLENDER PULSE ALL THE INGREDIENTS WITH
A HANDFULL OF CRUSHED ICE. POUR DIRECTLY
INTO A VOLUPTUOUS BALLOON GLASS.

flaming cool britannia

$^1/_2$ blue curaçao

$^1/_2$ crème de framboise

$^1/_2$ sambuca

$^1/_2$ rum or vodka

.................mixing glass...strainer...shot glass.............

POUR A LAYER OF BLUE CURAÇAO THEN A LAYER OF CRÈME
DE FRAMBOISE. IN A MIXING GLASS STIR THE SAMBUCA AND
RUM, NO ICE, THEN STRAIN GENTLY OVER THE BLUE AND RED
LAYERS. THIS COCKTAIL CAN BE MADE TO FLAME IF DESIRED!

down under

1 pineapple juice

1 passion juice

dash lime juice

$^{1}/_{2}$ pisang ambon

1 white rum

$^{1}/_{2}$ blue curaçao

gooseberry to garnish

.................mixing glass...bar spoon...wide martini......

STIR THE PINEAPPLE, PASSION AND LIME JUICES INTO A WIDE
GLASS FULL OF ICE. SLIDE IN THE PISANG AMBON. IN A
MIXING GLASS STIR THE RUM AND BLUE CURAÇAO AND
POUR OVER THE BACK OF A SPOON TO FLOAT ON TOP.

kiss me kate

dash lime juice

I white rum

$^1/_2$ pisang ambon

$^1/_2$ blue curaçao

bitter lemon

star fruit, heart-shaped cherry to garnish

......shaker...strainer...highball...........

SHAKE AND STRAIN THE LIME, RUM AND PISANG AMBON INTO
A HIGHBALL FILLED WITH ICE. TOP UP WITH BITTER LEMON.
STIR GENTLY AND SLIDE IN THE BLUE CURAÇAO.

mint julep

a few fresh mint leaves crushed with sugar

2 bourbon

crushed ice

twist of orange, cherry to garnish

.....................spoon for crushing...tumbler..............

TEAR SOME FRESH MINT LEAVES INTO A GLASS. CRUSH THEM
WITH A TEASPOON OF SUGAR. ADD THE CRUSHED ICE AND
THEN THE BOURBON. STIR.

cosmopolitan

dash lemon juice

dash cranberry juice

dash cointreau

2 vodka

......................shaker...strainer...martini glass...........

SHAKE ALL THE INGREDIENTS AND STRAIN INTO A GLASS

long island iced tea

dash tequila

dash gin

dash vodka

dash rum

dash cointreau

dash lemon juice

cola

lemon and lime to garnish

...............................highball...............................

IN A HIGHBALL FULL OF ICE CUBES, GENTLY STIR THE
ALCOHOL AND THE LEMON JUICE THEN TOP UP WITH COLA.

pink lady

dash grenadine

1 lemon juice

2 gin

................shaker...strainer...martini glass..............

SHAKE ALL INGREDIENTS TOGETHER
AND STRAIN INTO A FINE MARTINI GLASS.

champagne cocktail

sugar lump

Angostura bitters

dash cognac

champagne

orange to garnish

...................champagne flute or coupe...................

PLACE A SUGAR CUBE AT THE BOTTOM OF A CHAMPAGNE GLASS
STEEP THE SUGAR CUBE IN ANGOSTURA BITTERS,
ADD THE COGNAC AND TOP UP WITH CHAMPAGNE.

b52

$^1/_2$ grand marnier

$^1/_2$ baileys

$^1/_2$ kalhúa

.............................bar spoon....shot glass................

POUR THE KAHLÚA INTO A GLASS. THEN POUR THE BAILEYS,
THEN THE GRAND MARNIER OVER THE BACK OF A BAR SPOON
TO FLOAT ON TOP, IT CAN BE MADE TO FLAME IF DESIRED.

vodkatini

1 dry martini vermouth

2 vodka

twist of lemon or stuffed olive to garnish

...............mixing glass...strainer...martini glass...........

IN A MIXING GLASS STIR THE MARTINI AND VODKA OVER ICE.

STRAIN INTO A MARTINI GLASS.

blue lagoon

2 vodka

dash blue curaçao

1 lemon juice

lemon or star fruit to garnish

....................shaker...strainer...cocktail glass..............

SHAKE ALL INGREDIENTS WITH ICE CUBES.

STRAIN INTO A COCKTAIL GLASS.

sea breeze

2 vodka

2 cranberry juice

2 grapefruit juice

lime to garnish

.........................highball.........................

ADD ALL INGREDIENTS TO A HIGHBALL FILLED WITH ICE.

STIR GENTLY.

harvey wallbanger

1 vodka

½ galliano

orange juice

orange to garnish

.... highball ....

TO A HIGHBALL FULL OF ICE, ADD THE VODKA AND ORANGE
JUICE. STIR AND GENTLY ADD THE GALLIANO.

sex on the beach

I vodka

$^{1}/_{2}$ peach schnapps

dash grenadine

orange juice

lemon, lime, cherry to garnish

......................shaker...strainer..highball..................

ADD ALL INGREDIENTS TO A HIGHBALL FULL OF ICE AND STIR

OR

SHAKE ALL INGREDIENTS AND STRAIN INTO A GLASS OVER ICE.

mai tai

1 ¹/₂ white rum

¹/₂ grenadine syrup

¹/₂ lime cordial

dash orgeat syrup

dash lemon juice

¹/₂ dark rum

cherry, pineapple, mint leaf to garnish

.....................shaker...strainer...highball.....................

SHAKE ALL INGREDIENTS EXCEPT THE DARK RUM.
STRAIN OVER ICE CUBES INTO A HIGHBALL THEN
GENTLY SLIDE THE RUM OVER THE TOP.

bloody mary

I vodka

dash lemon juice

celery salt

tabasco

tomato juice

Worcestershire sauce

lemon, celery stick, ground black pepper to garnish

.... highball ....

GENTLY STIR ALL INGREDIENTS IN A HIGHBALL
OVER ICE CUBES.

caipirinhia

fresh pieces of lime

white sugar

ice

2 cachaca rum

..................spoon for crushing...tumbler..................

ADD THE LIME TO A TUMBLER WITH A TEASPOON OF SUGAR.
CRUSH TOGETHER. ADD THE ICE AND POUR IN THE CACHACA
RUM. STIR GENTLY BUT WELL.

white russian

1 kalhúa

1 vodka

$^1/_2$ fresh cream to float on top

..................bar spoon...tumbler or wide bowl..............

IN A TUMBLER FULL OF ICE, POUR IN THE VODKA AND
KALHÚA. STIR GENTLY. POUR THE CREAM OVER THE BACK OF A
BAR SPOON TO FLOAT ON TOP OF THE COCKTAIL.

moscow mule

1 vodka

$^1/_2$ lemon juice

ginger beer

lemon and lime to garnish

..........highball..........

POUR THE VODKA, LEMON JUICE AND GINGER BEER INTO A
HIGHBALL FULL OF ICE. STIR TOGETHER GENTLY.

laurent's tips

always chill glasses before use

unless otherwise specified, a shaker
and a mixing glass are always
filled with ice cubes

sliding the liquid
over the back of a bar spoon
to float on top of the cocktail
achieves perfect layers every time

laurent's tips

for the sugar rim **twist** the top of the
glass in a halved fresh lime then dip in white sugar.

keep vodka in **arctic** conditions

you can always **invent** your own cocktails
choose your favourite taste, colour, glass
and garnish and **voilà**

presentation is everything

cocktails prepared by laurent giraud-dumas
of the lanesborough hotel